MONTESSORI SENSORIAL

*New Montessori Sensorial Activities to Cultivate Learning
In the Classroom and the Home*

**Stacy Sanders
Certified Montessori Guide**

Published by Iditatran Press (USA) 948 Hudson Street, New York, NY 10014, Iditatran Press (Australia) Iditatran Press 19489 Wollumburah St. Sydney NSW, Australia, (Canada) edition Iditatran, 2010, 39 Rue De Filbraet, Montreal, Quebec, Canada, M4P 24, (England) 39 Brighton, F2CR OLA

IDITATRAN PRESS

Foreword

During my years as both a Certified Montessori Teacher and a caregiver, I received numerous requests from parents for more information outlining practical methods to facilitate their children's development in a simplified, condensed manner that honored the Montessori way. The result is this book. I have restricted this material to only the most comprehensive and applicable lessons for parents, parents to be, and guardians. I Include fundamentals and ideas taken directly from my hours in the classroom, my time as a nanny, my personal studies, and from insights shared with others dedicated to the tradition. Happy teaching!

Sensorial Contents

Theory
Sensorial Material
Movement
Group Lessons for Movement in the Classroom
Games
Three Period Lesson of Sequin
Example

Exercises

Sense of Sight
Visual Discrimination of Dimension
Montessori Solid Cylinders
The Montessori Pink Tower
The Montessori Long Stair
Montessori Knobless Cylinders
Discrimination of Color
Montessori Color Tablets
Auditory Sense
Montessori Sound Boxes
Bells
Tactile Sense
Montessori Rough and Smooth Touch Boards
Rough and Smooth Tablets
Fabrics
Smelling Boxes and Bottles
Thermic Sense
Thermic Bottles
Thermic Tablets
Baric Sense
Baric Tablets

The most marvelous aspect of the child is that he is an acute observer who sees things we cannot imagine he could have seen. How peculiar then, that we believe we must use bright colors, exaggerated gestures, and loud voices to attract his attention. What we do not know is that the child has a great capacity for observation and absorbs not only images of things, but relationships among things and is greatly advanced when we are least aware of it. -Maria Montessori, Child in the Family

Sensorial materials are designed to help the process of classification, and to enhance the skills of observation, isolate order, internalize skills of differences and similarities. To lend a child to a clear state of idea. The seeds planted in the mind can be transferred to the environment, therefore allowing possibilities for wider exploration. The ability to arrive at clear abstractions makes for clarity of the intellect. They grasp abstractness in a concrete form and then link it to foundations they have. The ability to classify clearly produces an orderly mind. Because classification is a function of order, the clearer the mind, the greater the possibility to communicate with others. This is a result of working with sensory materials. The child will not merely gain the ability to distinguish qualities in objects, but the materials to form an orderly mind.

Refinement of the senses follows this basic developmental order:

1. Perception of differences/recognition of contrast (sorting).
2. Perception of similarities/recognition of identities (matching).
3. Discrimination between extreme ends of the spectrum (preparation for grading).
4. Perception of minute differences between similar objects (grading).
5. Recall of sensory perceptions (memory games)

Materials Characteristics

Left to Right
Top to Bottom
Simple to Complex
Growth to Refined
Large to Small
Isolation to Combination
Single to Multiple
Indirect to Direct
External to Internal
Practical to Developmental
Known to Unknown

Fundamental Preparation for Exercises

1. Observe the child.
2. Evaluate the child's actions, needs, and interests.
3. Choose appropriate material that will continue the child's self-development.
4. Confirm that the learning materials are properly stored and in good repair.
5. Provide an uncluttered table or floor space.
6. Invite the child and request her consent for a demonstration.
7. If an apron is needed, show child where to get it and when to put it on.
8. Have child wash hands.
9. Show child where material is kept on shelf.
10. Name the material.
11. Show the child how to carry necessary materials to his workspace.
12. Seat the child comfortably, teacher to sit on child's dominant side, to perform actions with maximum visibility.
13. Slowly, clearly, and harmoniously lay out material in an orderly, functional manner.
14. Perform exercise with a sense of personal involvement. Be interesting, but don't over dramatize.
15. Uncover the main point of the exercise and the purpose of the material at hand.
Perform the demonstration with a sensible attempt and non-verbal communication.
16. Highlight important points by pausing or slowing down and by giving other visual gestures.
17. Evaluate the child's interests continuously and by making necessary adjustments.
18. Keep in mind the exercise ought to be challenging enough to cultivate interest and involvement, but not cause withdrawal by becoming too challenging.
19. Invite the child to repeat the lesson. If the child wishes to repeat, remain with him throughout the first attempt, be attentive, but do not intrude.

Point of Interest

*A specific point of interest may be shown to alert the child's attention to the process. These points should pertain to the learning materials at hand.
*Different children will need different doorways through which to begin an activity.
*The first presentation is not the opportunity to show or discuss all interesting variations or possible applications. Remember the value of isolation or difficulty.
*Permit the child the opportunity for self-discovery.

Control of Error

*Control of error is a specific feedback response relating to this material and it gives the child clues to his degree of accuracy. The control of error is unique to each activity, and is generally the simplest way to gauge if an action or answer is correct or incorrect.

Hands and Movement

The hand is the instrument of the intellect. –Maria Montessori

A child has the greatest concentration ability when the hand is involved. Movement is an expression of the psyche, the inner life of the child. While the child is born with the potential ability for the human movement, he must acquire coordinated movement through his own effort. Through sensorial material, the child acquires coordinated movement. Between the ages of 0-3, construction of movement is extremely important. Coordinated movement is necessary for the development of personality. In the first years of life, the burgeoning intellect of the child has a need for motor activity; to build itself and to shape its environment and to ascribe its surroundings with unique meaning.

In the case of classroom learning, the hand must always be free to move, as the child has great concentration when the hand is involved in an activity. Deep concentration, which is a natural tendency for the child, only comes from movement of the hand. This is why we must furnish classrooms with materials which engage the hand.

Group Lessons or Movement

For the degree of controlled movement, look for hand control, hand-eye coordination, and whether or not they are able to move without incident. When you're working with groups, as opposed to just observing, the aim is the control of movement, order, bodily activity, and interest in achieving exact movement and activity. To achieve the state where bodily activities are directed by will, there must be an aim behind the activities, not just movement. The lessons that follow focus on:

Collected Group – An entire class (8-30 students)
Group – Small numbers within class (2-5 students is ideal)
Individual.

Three Period Lesson of Seguin

"However desirable it may be to furnish a sense of education as a basis for intellectual ideas, it is never the less adversely at the same time to associate the language with perceptions." –Maria Montessori

Language serves as one of the child's major links with her world. Some researchers believe the development of language begins as early as in the womb. Maria Montessori focused on the period between ages 2½-6 years as the sensitive period for language development. Édouard Séguin was the founder on this idea, by recognizing a 3-step process in the mastery of information. The Three Period Lesson is utilized with the child in assisting in learning various names of objects, categories, classes, and characteristics of objects to be found in his environment. Following Seguin, Maria Montessori advised lessons be given in 3 stages, or *Periods*. That may be thought of as *Association, Recognition*, and *Recall*.

1st Period – Name or identify the association of the sensory perception with the child present. For example: colors. The adult pointing to an object and says: "This is red." This period is also called *Personal Introduction*.

2nd Period – Recognition of an object corresponding to the object's name. The adult may say "Show me red, or show me blue." It is imperative to repeat several variations of the questioning phase. For example: "Hand me blue, point to yellow." You may also ask them to point to materials. For example: "Put the green here."

3rd Period – Recall. Remembering the name corresponding with the object. The adult points to or touches the material and says, "What is this?" This is the period for the test. Mastery is reached when the child can identify the object at will, without any reminder from the First or Second Period. Often, the adult will end the lesson at the first or second period, especially for children under 4.

Presuppositions

1. Montessori emphasizes that there is a period that comes before the Three Period's of Seguin. This is the period when the child works alone with the sensorial material and experiences different sensory stimuli without verbal interruption. This period of acquisition should precede the Three Periods of Seguin." Ann Nubert, from *A Way of Learning*.

2. When presenting an object, move it to the front of the child with the rest of the immediate visual field cleared.

3. The senses should be involved when appropriate. Feeling, hearing, or smelling the object when presenting it.

4. Proceed to the next period only when you are assured of the child's success and confidence in the previous period.

5. Vary the order of the objects presented. This helps to differentiate between the child who actually knows the names: "Put the circle here, put the square there."

6. Be sure to spend sufficient time on the Second Period.

7. Exemplary pronunciation by the teacher is important in helping the child develop clear speech and exact vocabulary.

8. All three periods do not need to be done in the same setting. Stop (or pause) when the child first begins to show error. Return to the previous period when repeating the lesson.

Montessori Solid Cylinders

Ages: 2½ - 3½

Materials: Four blocks containing ten cylinders with knobs, each fitting into its respective hole and differing in dimension.

A. Each with the same diameter, rising in height successively from short to tall. Each differing in a single aspect: height.

B. Each growing in diameter successively from thin to thick, while their height remains equal throughout. Each differs in two dimensions: width and breadth.

C. Each growing successively in diameter from small to large, while diminishing in height from tall to short. Each differs in 3 dimensions: while the diameter increases, the height decreases.

D. Each growing in diameter from small to large, while at the same time rising in height like A. Each differs in 3 dimensions: width, breadth, and height, but all increase regularly, if one proceeds from the smallest.

Presentation:

1. Invite child, name the lesson, and show where work is located.
2. Select a solid cylinder set from the shelf and set it carefully on table.
3. Remove the cylinders form the box, one-by-one, from largest to smallest.
4. Line the cylinders up in front of the box randomly.
5. Place the smallest back in its place first and then continue randomly.
6. Bring back to the shelf.

Exercise:

1. Do the cylinder blocks individually at the presentation.
2. Work with two cylinder blocks in a parallel position, placing cylinders inside.
3. Work with three cylinder blocks in a triangle position, placing cylinders inside.
4. Work with all four sets in a square position, place cylinders inside.

Purpose:

1. Direct aim: Visual discrimination of dimension.
2. Indirect aim: Preparation of fingers for writing.

Control Error: Within material.

Language: 3rd period on:

Block A- short/tall
Block B- thick/thin
Block C- large/small and comparative and superlative forms
Block D- large/small

Notes:

1. If the child begins to place cylinders in random order, allow him to do so. Repeat presentation of blocks individually with the following preparation if possible: B, C, D, A.
2. This lesson should always be performed on a table.
3. It is important to emphasize matching, not trial and error.
4. Don't teach the child grading. This will come later by himself as he works with the material.
5. Two or three children may work on the triangle and square formations if they can work without competition.

Montessori Pink Tower

Ages: 2½ -3.

Materials:

1. Ten pink cubes differing in length, breadth, and height. Their sizes grow progressively in the algebraic series of the third power.

2. Starting from the smallest, which in size is 1 cubic cm, 8 of this would make the next largest cube, and 27 of the first would make the third cube, etc.

Presentation:

1. Invite child, prepare mat, name lesson, and show where work is located.
2. Walk over to pink tower and begin placing cubes randomly on the mat.
3. Begin stacking tower from largest cubes to smallest cubes.
4. Take apart again, placing cubes on mat.
5. Put away properly on its stand, beginning with the largest, stacking the tower successively.

Exercise:

1. As presentation.
2. After much experience building the tower, build with two sides and one corner matching.
3. After it's built in this manner, demonstrate how the smallest block fits around the edge of every other block.

Purpose:

1. Direct Aim- visual discrimination of the difference in dimension and muscular control of the hand and arm.
2. Indirect Aim- education of voluntary movement, preparation for the hand, preparation for relative sizes, preparing for the mathematical mind, preparation for volume and cubing numbers to the third power.

Language:

Three Period Lesson on large and small using largest to smallest cubes to illustrate contrast and their comparative and superlative forms.

Montessori Long Stair

Ages: 2½ - 3½

Materials:

Ten red rods differing only in length. The smallest rod is 10 cm long and each succeeding rod differs from the preceding rod by the length of the first. No separate names are given to the rods.

Presentation:

1. Invite child, prepare the mat, name work, and show where work is located.
2. Place the shortest rod on the mat.
3. Carry the next two rods and place on the mat.
4. Continue getting rods one at a time until all rods are on mat.
5. Sit on child's dominant side.
6. Choose the longest rod and place it at the top of the mat (display length.)
7. Choose the second longest rod and place it neatly beside the first rod.
8. Choose the third longest rod and place it neatly beside the second rod, continue in this manner until all rods are standing.
9. When finished, begin carrying each rod back to the shelf, tallest to shortest.
10. Rename the work.

Purpose:

1. Direct Aim: Visual discrimination of length.
2. Indirect Aim: Preparation for number work.

Control of Error: Visual disharmony.

Language: A Three Period Lesson on:

A. Long and short.
B. Comparative and superlative forms.

Purpose of Games:

A. Application of Language.

Montessori Broad Stair

Ages: 2½ - 3½

Materials:

Ten prisms (or blocks) of identical length, (traditionally) brown in color, differing in breadth and height. Each prism grows progressively in the alphabetical series of the second power i.e. 4 of the first to make the second. 9 of the first to make the third, etc.

Presentation:

1. Invite child, prepare the mat, name the lesson, show where the work is located.
2. Carefully bring the smallest prism to the mat using pincer grip. Randomly bring all pieces one by one.
3. Place the largest prism starting on the edge of the mat, exactly halfway down.
4. Continue placing prisms in a row (largest to smallest) until they are all neatly lined up.
5. After all prisms are set, take a moment to observe complete structure.
6. Put away prisms one at a time, beginning with the largest.

Purpose:

Direct visual discrimination of dimension, indirect muscular development of the grip, and preparation of the mathematical mind.

Control of Error: Visual disharmony.

Language: Three Period Lesson on broad to narrow and their comparative and superlative.

Montessori Color Tablets

Ages: 2½ - 3½

Materials:

1. A box containing six tablets of lightly enameled woods. One color per pair of red, blue, and yellow.
2. A box containing twenty-two tablets, one pair of each: red, orange, yellow, green, blue, violet, pink, grey, brown, black, and white.
3. One box with 9 compartments, each containing 7 tablets in graduations of each of the above colors.

Color Presentation: Box One

1. Name lesson.
2. Child and teacher wash hands.
3. Show child where tablets are located on the shelf.
4. Gently remove lid and place it to the side.
5. Grasp side of tablet on wooden part and line tablets (turn horizontally) on top of the table from left to right.
6. Close the box, take the first (color order doesn't matter) and touch it lightly. "I'd like to find one just like one."
7. Place tablet (vertically turned) to the left and match. Repeat with remaining two. 8. Place matches beneath the first.

Note: If child has the ability, continue with the second box in the same lesson.

Color Presentation: Box Two

1. Begin by placing secondary colors randomly on table.
2. Remove 3 pairs.
3. Line them up along across the top of the table.
4. "I'd like to find a color just like this one."
5. Place matches to the left, vertically turned.
6. After pairing the first 3, ask if she would like to try more colors.
7. If yes, take out 3 or more and continue.
8. Put away in an alternating pattern in the box when finished.

Exercise: The child mixes and pairs tablets. If child's comprehension is slow, begin exercise again by presenting red, yellow, blue.

Purpose: Direct Aim: Sensorial training providing child with the key to the world of color.

Control of Error: Visual disharmony.

Language: After much practice, use a Three Period Lesson to present language. After box three, give a Three Period Lesson on darkest to lightest, plus their comparative and superlative forms.

Games: Usually these games come after language is given. Games are never used to interest a child in material. Only after a child is competent with it.

Note: According to the National Eye Institute, color blindness affects approximately 1 in 12 males, and 1 in 200 females. If a child seems to be developing slowly in this activity (especially if they are a boy) they may simply be color-blind. Be especially vigilant in watching for this, as there is no other manner by which to differentiate tablets.

Montessori Sound Boxes

Ages: 3-6

Material: Two boxes each containing six cylinders, one red set, one blue set, Each cylinder has a small quantity of beads (or other material) inside, but the sizes of the material varies with each pair, so that when they are shaken, a different sound is produced. The sound should be graded from loud to very soft.

Presentation:

1. Invite child, name lesson, show where work is located on shelf.
2. Bring both red and blue boxes to the table one at a time (demonstrate how to carry carefully with thumb over the lid).
3. Place boxes side-by-side on the table with blue on the left, red on the right. Leave a space in-between the boxes. Remove 3 blue cylinders one by one. Line them up vertically next to the blue box. Repeat with the red sound box.
4. Shake the first blue cylinder next to your ear in a gentle up and down motion. Tell the child: "Let's find one that sounds just like this one."
5. Shake again, then place it along the bottom of the table. Select a blue sound box and shake. Listen with great care. If it is not the match, shake your head. Shake the original one again and then try another red. Repeat until the match is found.
6. Place the matching cylinders side-by-side to the left of the table.
7. Shake the next blue, place at the bottom of the table, then a red. Ask child if she would like to try.
8. Continue shaking and matching, place the matches under the first match to the left of your table.
9. Once the matches have been made and lined up, check each pair for accuracy, beginning with the top pair.
10. Replace in box, one at a time beginning with blue. Put the first away at the top of the box, the second at the bottom.

Exercise:

1. As presentation.
2. Grading: teacher grades the first set. Child then grades the red, using the teachers set to check. During this time teacher is teaching comparative and superlative: louder, loudest, softer, softest.

Purpose: Training of auditory sense.

Control of Error: Within the material. When matching, the error will show up in the last pair. For grading, the teacher's graded set is the control.

Language: Use a Three Period Lesson to present loud and soft. Give the positive loud/soft before grading, and the comparative and superlative during grading.

Games:

1. Matching: Divide set at opposite sides of the room.
2. Grading: Child can differentiate comparative of loud, soft.

Rough and Smooth Touch Boards

Ages: 2½- 3½

Material: Four Rectangular Boards

A. Board divided into two equal squares, one covered with rough sandpaper, the other covered with smooth paper or polished wood.
B. Board divided into eleven narrow partitions, alternating smooth and rough.
C. Board divided into eleven arrow partitions, graded in rough surfaces.
D. Board divided into eleven narrow partitions, graded in smooth surfaces.

Presentation:

1. Invite child, name lesson, show where work is located on the shelf.
2. Pour water into a dish, dip index and middle fingers in water, dry.
3. Invite child to stroke lightly from top to bottom, starting with smooth touch board.
4. Put on blindfold to isolate sensation.
5. Move on to the next board.
6. Put work away.
7. Dump water.
8. Replace washcloth.
9. Return to shelf.

Exercise: As presentation.

Purpose: Direct aim: to develop tactile control of muscular action by lightness of touch needed. Indirect aim: preparation for writing due to up and down motions, lightness of touch, and the left-to-right movement.

Language: Given with presentation as a Three Period Lesson. Boards C and D: Comparative/ superlative of rough and smooth.

Notes: 1.Touch boards are a preliminary exercise for all touch exercises. Therefore, it's important to begin early and give to child as soon as he has hand control.

Rough and Smooth Tablets

Ages: 2½-3½

Materials:

1. Box Containing 6 pairs of tablets varying in their surfaces. They can be comprised of cardboard or wood. All should be uniform in size, and covered with different qualities of paper: shiny, sooth, dull, rough, (drawing paper, plain cardboard, and various grades of sandpaper.) There must be two of each kind. If feasible, the color of the surface of each pair should differ somewhat from other parts.
2. Blindfold (optional but recommended).
3. Small tray, bowl, pitcher, and rough cloth.

Presentation:

1. Invite child, name lesson, show where it's located on shelf.
2. Wash hands.
3. Lay out the six boards across table.
4. Bring the first (on the left) towards you and trace from top to bottom.
5. "Let's find one that feels just like this one." Place matches side by side to the left corner.
6. Pull the next tablet toward you and repeat.
7. If the selected pair is not a match, replace and try the next one.
8. Place pairs under first match (3 pairs).
9. Take out the rest of the tablets. Repeat.
10. Put tablets back in box randomly, alternating top/bottom.

Note: Once child is adept at matching pairs, you may wish to introduce blindfold.

Exercise: As presentation.

Purpose:

Direct aim: develop tactile sense and control of action.
Indirect aim: preparation for writing by degrees of touch and development of tactile (mainly wrist) actions.

Control of Error: Grades of roughness and\or matching colors.

Fabrics

Ages: 2½ - 3½

Material:

1. Two sets of pairs of different qualities of materials. One is finer, smoother, and silkier than the other. The other is made of rougher, coarser, and thicker materials. Other than these characteristics, all other qualities are the same. Each piece should be 6 x 6 inches square.
2. Blindfold.
3. Small tray, pitcher, bowl, and rough cloth.

Presentation:

1. Invite child.
2. Name work and show where it's located on the shelf.
3. Sanitize hands.
4. Lay each square across mat beginning at left side.
5. Pull one towards you and feel with 4 fingers. "I'm looking for one that feels the same as this one."
6. Feel each fabric square until match is found. Then pair up by placing it on top of one other.
7. Choose next square. Repeat. When paired, place back in basket randomly.
8. Return to shelf with child.

Exercise:

1. As presentation.
2. Have child close eyes. Give 2 different pieces of cloth, one in each hand. Select one and ask child to feel if the other is the same. If yes, take both cloths and put aside together. If not, help them clear space to try another. Give next cloth in right hand and ask if it feels the same. If 'yes' place the pair together. Continue until all cloths are paired. Remove blindfold to see if pairing is correct.
3. After much experience with fabrics, blindfold and have child feel 2 different cloths and ask, "Do these feel the same?" If 'No', place to the side, give child more cloths. One of which matches the first pair.

Purpose: To furnish child the opportunity of refining sense of touch.

Note: Pairs should be a different color.

Language: Give names of fabrics using Three Period Lesson.

Notes:

1. 5 pairs of material per box. Keep laundered, and if possible, change up material.
2. It is not necessary for teacher to introduce all the exercises, children can work together.
3. After experience with rough fabrics, present smooth and follow in same progression. Some steps may not be necessary.

Smelling Bottles

Ages: 3½+

Materials:

1. 7 pairs of boxes or bottles containing various substances with distinct perfumes such as essential oils, fragrances, and light perfumes. Recommended: Rose water, Bergamot fragrance, Lavender, Vanilla, Peppermint oil, Clove, Frankincense, Myrrh, Amber etc.*
2. Use 1-2 drops per bottle, bottles should be sealable, and small enough for small hands to manage.
3. (Optional but recommended) Tray to transfer bottles

*Essential oils are strongly preferred over artificial or chemical scents. Avoid blends.

Presentation:

1. Show child where bottles are located on shelf.
2. Mix bottles and invite child to help you transfer bottles.
3. "I want to find one that smells just like this one."
4. Allow child to smell each bottle, and find the match.
5. When child makes a match, confirm their selections, praise, and put matches together on tray.

Exercise:

1. As presentation.
2. Matching classified scents.

Purpose: To cultivate awareness of various smells.

Control of error: Mark bottoms of bottles with letters to confirm that you are correct.

Language: Name aromas within each bottle using a Three Period Lesson.

Games:

1. Smell one bottle and search for something with same smell in environment.

2. Smell object and search for something in environment with similar smells.
3. Explore outdoors and try to find 5 things with unique smells. Flowers are an obvious choice. Many herbs also have unique smells.
4. Demonstrate the role that the nose has by asking child to hold her nose as she tastes something. Explain the role that the nose plays in taste.

Exploring Taste

Ages: 3½+

Materials: (per student)

1. 1 tray.
2. 4 small plates.
3. Four flavors:
A. Sour: (Lemon or lime squeezed in water)
B. Bitter: (Small piece of endive, chicory, chard, or dandelion)
C. Sweet: (1/2 teaspoon Pure Maple Syrup, or 2 sugar cubes)
D. Salty: (1-2 potato chips)

Notes: Due to allergens and restrictive diets, it is important to clear this exercise with parents and\or guardians before giving students any food. In addition, it is also important to encourage your child to rinse out their mouth after every sample.

Language: Four fundamental tastes: Sour, Bitter, Sweet, Salty. Employ the Three Period Lesson.

Thermic Bottles

Age: 3½+

Material:
1. Eight small receptacles containing water of the follow temperatures:

A. Room Temperature: To prepare water for Bottle A use room temperature water.
B. 2 at approximately 10 degrees warmer (slightly warmer) To prepare water for Bottle B use warm tap water.
C. 2 at approximately 10 degrees cooler (slightly cooler) To prepare water for Bottle C use cool tap water.
D. 2 at approximately 20 degrees colder (cold water) To prepare water for Bottle D use ice cubes, and remove right before exercise.

1. Mark the room temperature bottles with a red or pink line to help the child differentiate them. Mark all bottles on the bottom to serve as the control of error.
2. Tray.
3. Paper Towels (to dry fingers).

Espresso cups work well for this exercise.

Presentation:

1. Invite child.
2. Name lesson and show where it's located on the shelf.
3. "We are going to use our fingers to feel."
4. Line bottles up in 2 vertical rows next to box.
5. Randomize bottles.
6. Starting with bottle A: "feel this one, I'd like to find one that feels just like this one."

Exercise:
1. As presentation.
2. Matching, grading.

Notes: Grading is done after child has been given language of hot and cold. Teacher grades one set of bottles as hot, warmer, cool, cooler.

Purpose: To develop the thermic sense.

Language: Three Period Lesson: before grading: language is hot/cold/during grading: hot, warmer, cool, cooler.

Notes: Younger children may need markings on top of bottles to help them.

Baric Tablets

Ages: 2½-3½+

Materials:

Three boxes, each containing six wooden tablets. Each set of tablets is of a different wood from the other 2 sets, so that they differ in weight as well as color from each other. They are of light, medium, and heavy weight.

Presentation:

1. Invite child.
2. Name work and show where it's located on the shelf.
3. Wash hands.
4. Carry the 2 boxes one at a time to the table and line them up vertically on the table. Set the darkest one closet to you.
5. One by one remove tablets from heavy box. When empty, pull empty container at the top.
6. Pull lighter tablet toward you. Place heavy one flat in left hand and light one in right.
7. Weight them together moving gently up and down.
8. Put heaviest away in box closet.
9. Switch boxes, and put light away.
10. Return to shelf.

Exercise:

1. As presentation (light/heavy).
2. Same as presentation. Use light and medium, medium, heavy.
3. Mix all three sets into three piles.
4. Various heavies and lights: The same as presentation, but have him close his eyes. "We are going to feel heavy and light." Give him one of each. Deposit one in heavy pile and one in light pile.

Purpose:

Development of baric sense. Blindfold helps to direct attention to weight of tablet.

Control of Error: Different colors of wood.

Language: After much experience, use a Three Period Lesson to present, heavy, medium, and light.

Discrimination of Grains

Materials:

1. 1 tray with a number of saucers on each of which is a little heap of a grains: wheat, barley rice, lentils, peas, beans, coffee beans, mustard seeds, sesame seeds etc.
2. One empty dish.

Presentation:

1. Invite Child.
2. Name work. Show where work is located on the shelf.
3. Begin with saucer in left hand. Give to child. Have her touch grains with hand, encourage her to smell it.
4. Repeat with next saucer, feel it, smell it, take note of size.
5. Repeat above steps until all saucers have been experienced.
6. Ask permission to blindfold child.
7. Guide her hand to feel each grain in tray and then have her match objects from that tray to proper saucers.
8. Return to shelf.

Notes: Start younger children on larger objects (buttons, seeds).

Exercise: As presentation. Introduce other trays as interest grows.
Direct aim: Development of sterognostic sense and refinement of hand movement.

Control of Error: Visual, when child sees containers.

Language: No language is given with this exercise, unless child inquires about grains themselves. If he does, explain them.

Mystery Bag

Material:

1. An aesthetic bag containing approximately a dozen items. Examples of contents could be: a key, a marble, a pinecone, a stone, a walnut, an avocado pit, a thimble, an eraser, a pen cap, a spool of thread, etc.
2. A blindfold.

Presentation:

1. Admire beauty of mystery bag.
2. Begin with objects child may recognize, feel around in the bag.
3. Slowly pull out objects, allow child to observe, and place them in front of child.
4. Return objects to bag.
5. Invite child to take a turn.

Exercise: As presentation.

Purpose: Training of stereognostic sense and the power to visualize mentally.

Control of Error: Other children, if eyes are closed: open eyes.

Ages: 3-6

Notes:

After experience with familiar objects, introduce new objects in the bag.
Children may work alone or with others.

Geometric Solids

Age: 2½+

Materials:

Individual solid geometrical forms such as a:
A) Sphere
B) Ovoid
C) Ellipsoid
D) Rectangular prism
E) Cone
F) Cube
G) Triangular pyramid
H) Square pyramid
I) Cylinder
J) Globe

Presentation:

1. Invite child.
2. Name lesson.
3. Show where work is located.
Begin with only 3 contrasting solids: sphere, cylinder, cube remove each basket, one by one, feel each solid carefully and solly with complete hand enclosure.
4. Set each down across the top of the mat.
5. Pick up the sphere, name it, and feel it again. Have child feel. Replace at the top of the mat.
6. Repeat with the cylinder and cube.
7. Continue with a Three Period Lesson on the names of the solids.
8. Carefully put each back in basket and return to shelf.
9. If child displays interest, retrieve others from the shelf.
10. Introduce all other cubes in later lessons, in accordance with how quickly they are grasping the concepts.

Exercise:

1. Take shapes the child knows, put theses shapes in a basket, cover with cloth, reach in and retrieve one, say its name.

2. Introduce bases. Begin with 3 contrasting bases for solids. For example: square rectangle, cycle. Remove solid from basket and match it with base. Turn solid on various sides to see if it's a

match. Child may then experiment to see which solids fit on which bases.

Purpose: Direct aim to make child aware of the solid geometrical shapes that surround him. Indirect aim: Preparation for geography.

Control of error: Other children, bases.